MEADOW OAKS SCHOOL

Birthday Book Club

Title: _____JAPANESE SPORTS CARS_____

Given by: _____MATTHEW BAILEY_____

Grade: _____2_____ Date: _____APRIL 4, 1998_____

Meadow Oaks School
23456 Mulholland
Calabasas, Calif. 91302

JAPANESE SPORTS CARS
SPEED AND STYLE

by
JERRY CRAVEN
and
LINDA CRAVEN

THE ROURKE CORPORATION, INC.
Vero Beach, FL 32964

ACKNOWLEDGMENTS

Many people helped in the writing of this book. I am especially grateful to Mark Brantley for his help with the Nissan Z series; Douglas J. Westhoff for help with the Mitsubishi 3000 GT; Art Garner for help with the Lexus sports coupes; and Stephanie J. Croull of Mazda Motor of America for her help with the RX-7, the MX-3, the MX-6 and the Miata. Thanks also go to Tracey Hawk and Betty Jackson, both of Mazda Motor of America, and to Cory Dupriest.

Library of Congress Cataloging-in-Publication Data

Craven, Linda.
    Japanese sports cars / by Linda Craven and Jerry Craven.
       p. cm. — (Car classics)
    Includes index.
    Summary: Provides a brief history of Japanese sports cars in the United States and describes the special features of the most popular models.
    ISBN 0-86593-256-5
    1. Sports cars – Juvenile literature. 2. Automobiles – Japan – Juvenile literature. [1. Sports cars – Japan.
2. Automobiles – Japan.] I. Craven, Jerry. II. Title. III. Series: Car classics (Vero Beach, Fla.)
TL236.C72   1993
629.222 – dc20
                        93-14917
                        CIP
                        AC

CONTENTS

CHAPTER 1

NEW IDEAS FOR NEW CARS

The Acura NSX is called an "exotic" sports car because it is assembled by hand.

Japanese automakers are newcomers to the production of sports cars. Some, such as Nissan with its Z series, have produced sports cars for more than 20 years. A large number of them, though, have begun making sports cars only in the last few years.

This 1993 Nissan ZX convertible is part of the Z series of sports cars that dates back to 1969.

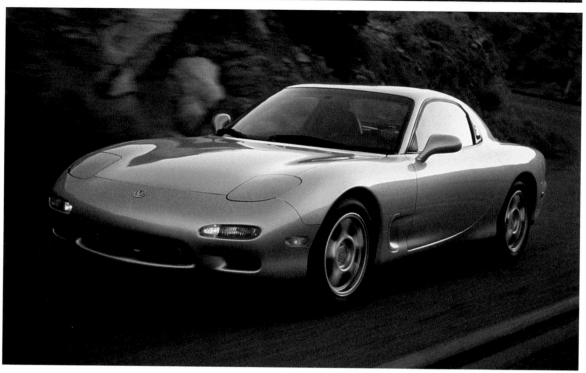

This Mazda RX-7 is powered by a rotary engine.

Most Japanese sports cars are built on highly-automated assembly lines. Japanese car builders like efficiency, and Japanese engineers like to design sports models with the latest high technology.

Few sports cars from anywhere in the world are built without the use of an assembly line conveyer belt. The Acura NSX is an exception. It is what sports car enthusiasts call an "exotic." This means it is a low-production car that is designed for speed, and it is hand-built.

Japanese sports cars have a number of things in common. All make use of sophisticated computer technology to make the car run better and with greater comfort. All are designed for both looks and stability at high speed. Most of them are built for American buyers.

Sports cars that Japanese builders offer to American drivers range from the tiny Miata roadster, to the Lexus 400 luxury coupe, to cars like the Mazda RX-7 R-1 that appeal mainly to race car purists. Most Japanese car makers try to appeal both to lovers of comfortable, sporty cars as well as to those interested mainly in sports car styling and speed.

CHAPTER 2

NISSAN: THE EARLY Z

This 1974 Datsun 260 Z fastback had a 2.6 liter engine.

When Nissan started selling cars in the United States, their cars were called *Datsuns*. The sporty Z series appeared in 1969. It was called a Datsun 240 Z, or just Z. The sports car had a 2.4 liter straight six engine that produced 150 horsepower and could go from zero to 60 in 8.7 seconds.

The 240 Z was so popular in the United States that demand was greater than supply. Customers who could get a new Z paid $3,526 for it. However, demand was so great that the *Kelly Bluebook* in 1970 rated a new Z at $4,000. People were paying more for a used Z than for a new one because the new Z was in short supply.

In the 1970s, the Z began a gradual change from a fast sports car to a more luxurious, less powerful car. The loss in power was due to new pollution control requirements in the United States. The 1974 260 Z had a 2.6 liter engine to help make up for power loss from emission control devices. In 1974, the Datsun Z offered a four-seater, and the wheelbase grew by 12 inches.

The 280 Z, begun in 1975, had to meet even tougher pollution control laws. So it offered more horsepower and torque with a fuel-injected engine.

The first turbocharged engine appeared in the 1980 280 ZX. It was called a GT, or a "grand touring" car. Nissan thought of it as a luxury car that could pass for a sports car.

American buyers welcomed the changes in the Z that made it bigger and more luxurious. It sold well, which meant that Nissan understood the market.

As with all cars in the Z series, the control panel of the 1991 Nissan 300 ZX was designed to be read at a glance.

CHAPTER 3

NISSAN: THE Z SERIES, STRUGGLING WITH SIZE

Left: This 1974 Datsun 260 Z was longer than previous models by 12 inches.

Nissan introduced a new body design in the 1983 300 ZX. It came with a 3.0 liter V-6 with a turbocharged option. Horsepower for the regular engine in the 300 ZX was 160. The turbo engine produced 200 horsepower.

The 1983 300 ZX moved the car more into the luxury line. In the next few years, sales dropped, and Nissan reconsidered the long, slow movement of the Z series from sportster to luxury car.

The result was the 1986 300 ZX. It put more emphasis on performance and less on luxury. The body became rounder. The engine became a 24-valve V-6 that produced 222 horsepower. To improve performance, the engine had a system to vary timing of the valves with engine speed.

Fumio Yoshida was one of the men who helped create the original 240 Z. He helped with the development of later models. During the era of the 300 ZX, he was a design executive. It was a goal of Yoshida to introduce into the 300 ZX series as much of the spirit of the original 240 Z as possible.

This 1993 Nissan 300 ZX continues Nissan's 1986 decision to return the Z from the luxury car it had become to its original image as a sports car.

Yoshida saw to it that the 1990 300 ZX had the look of a state-of-the-art sports car. For this model, the design team gave more attention than ever to aerodynamics. They wanted to reduce air drag and improve road stability. At the same time they sought a design that had the rounded, sleek look of the contemporary sportster.

CHAPTER 4

NISSAN: THE 300 ZX, SPORTS AND LUXURY MODELS

The original 240 Z appealed to the sports car purists. Then, in the decades of the 1970s and '80s, when the Z series became more a grand touring car, it developed a different following. With the attempt to get back to its roots as a sports car, the 300 ZX ran the risk of losing customers who wanted a sporty luxury car. Not wanting to lose either market, Nissan has tried to capture both by putting out four models of the 300 ZX.

The models look much alike. Two are two-seaters, built for those who think sports cars ought to sacrifice convenience for speed. The other two are four-seaters, for lovers of the Z series who like the cross between a grand touring car and a sports car.

This 1993 300 ZX was built for both comfort and speed.

*This 1991 300 ZX
has a rear seat.*

To improve handling, the 1993 300 ZX has a four-wheel steering system that is computer controlled. At low and high speeds, the rear wheels track as rear wheels do in cars without four-wheel steering. At medium speeds, though, when the driver turns the steering wheel sharply, a computer tells the rear wheels to steer the opposite way. This has the effect of pointing the car faster in the direction the driver is turning. Then, a fraction of a second later, the rear wheels line up normally again.

For the near future, Nissan will place its energy into making the Z series a high-tech sports car with models to appeal to lovers of the classic Z *and* lovers of sporty cars with the comfort of a grand touring car.

CHAPTER 5

MITSUBISHI: THE 3000 GT, SPEED AND CONTROL

Mitsubishi began production of the 3000 GT sports car in 1991. There are two versions of the 3000 GT. Both are marketed as a blend of comfort and power. The *GT* in the name marks it as a "grand touring" car, which implies luxury and comfort. The manufacturers refer to the 3000 GT as a "grand touring sports car."

The two models of the 3000 GT are the more expensive VR-4 and the SL. Both have the look of world-class sports cars. They have aerodynamic lines and subtle muscle bulges on the hood and front fenders. The 3000 GT models are two-seaters that emphasize driver and passenger comfort and provide a minimum of storage, as is typical of sports cars.

The super model, the VR-4, is fast. It has a 3.0 liter V-6 engine that will generate 300 horsepower. The car will go from zero to 60 in 5.6 seconds. Its top speed is 160 mph.

In addition to having power, the 3000 GT VR-4 has some high-tech engineering built into it that is unusual. Most impressive are its four-wheel steering and the way it deals with air currents at high speeds.

The bucket seats of the 3000 GT are designed to hold driver and passenger in place during high-speed cornering.

The spoiler mounted on the trunk of this 1993 3000 GT will automatically change angles at high speeds.

All four wheels respond to steering at speeds over 31 mph. The rear wheels do not steer much – just enough to help with high speed cornering.

At 50 mph, the rear wind stabilizer, or spoiler, across the back of the car changes position. It tilts 14 degrees, enough to make the wind press the back of the car harder to the road.

CHAPTER 6

MITSUBISHI: HIGH TECHNOLOGY IN THE 3000 GT

The Mitsubishi 3000 GT SL looks almost identical to its more expensive brother, the 3000 GT VR-4. The SL has a less powerful engine (see box) and a less luxurious interior. Also, the SL comes with an optional automatic transmission. The manual transmission option is the same as the VR-4, a five-speed stick shift.

The VR-4 has all-wheel drive, while the SL has front-wheel drive only. Also, on the SL, anti-lock brakes are an option. On the VR-4 they are standard.

The automatic transmission option on the SL is impressive. A computer watches driving style and adjusts shift timing for best performance. Also, the automatic has an overdrive for greater fuel efficiency.

This 1993 3000 GT VR-4 can go from zero to 60 in 5.6 seconds.

Mitsubishi	VR-4	SL
Engine type	90 degree V-6	90 degree V-6
Displacement	3.0 liters	3.0 liters
Horsepower	300 at 6000 rpm	222 at 6000 rpm
Torque	307 lb-ft at 4500 rpm	201 lb-ft at 4500 rpm
Drivetrain	full-time 4-wheel drive	front-wheel drive

The VR-4 engine is more powerful because of its twin turbochargers.

As with the 3000 GT SL, the VR-4 has a spoiler that tilts at high speeds to keep the car stable. Another bit of high technology that keeps the VR-4 stable is an electronically controlled suspension system. This system automatically adjusts the reaction rate of the car's three-way shock absorbers.

The VR-4 makes another use of computer technology in the brakes. Computer sensors watch the wheels for signs of wheel lock during braking. When they detect lock-up, which can cause the car to skid, the sensors signal a computerized system to pulse the brakes many times per second. The car can then stop safely without skidding.

The 1993 3000 GT comes with a stick shift or an automatic transmission.

CHAPTER 7

LEXUS: POWER AND COMFORT

The Lexus coupe has the look and power of a sports car. Its speedometer goes up to 160, and it accelerates like a racer. It has the compact and muscular design of a world-class sportster. The company that makes it refers to it as a *luxury sports coupe.*

The Lexus coupe comes in two models, the SC 300 and the SC 400. The difference is mainly in the engines. The SC 400 has a 4.0 liter, four-camshaft, 32-valve V-8 engine. The SC 300 has a 3.0 liter, twin-cam, 24-valve straight six engine.

Another difference is that the SC 300 comes with either a five-speed stick shift or a four-speed automatic transmission. The SC 400 comes only with automatic transmission.

The smooth lines and muscle bulges of the Lexus SC 400 suggest a powerful, even ride.

Motor Trend magazine selected the SC 400 as its 1992 Import Car of the Year. The magazine praised the car for its handling and speed and called it a luxury car. The SC 400, *Motor Trend* said, is "as good as the Mercedes-Benz 500 SL for half the price."

The designers of the Lexus tried to avoid preconceived ideas by avoiding drawings. Instead, they went from a sculpted model to a prototype, much as the designers of early Jaguars did. The final look of the car combines smooth lines with aerodynamics that keep the car steady and quiet even at high speeds.

The Lexus SC 300 differs from the SC 400 mainly in having a smaller engine.

CHAPTER 8

LEXUS: LUXURY SPORTS COUPE

Like all truly modern sports cars, the Lexus makes use of computers. A computer regulates such things as ignition timing, fuel injection and anti-lock brakes. On the SC 400 and on the SC 300 models with automatic transmissions, a computer interfaces engine and transmission. The driver can select *normal* or *power* modes for shifting, depending on driving style.

Many people refer to the SC 300 and SC 400 as luxury cars, though they look and drive like sports cars. They also have extras a sports car enthusiast might scorn. In the 1993 models, for example, a computer sensor gauges the amount of available light and automatically turns on the headlights when they are needed.

Lexus makes two four-door luxury sedans and a sports coupe. The sports model is on the right.

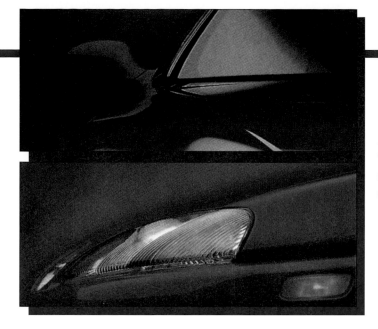

Lines of the Lexus coupe were designed for smooth air flow and for sleek appearance.

Also, both coupes are wired for a voice-activated phone system. The system will remember two different voices. This allows two people to give short vocal commands, and the phone will dial pre-programmed numbers. It is possible to call someone, talk and hang up without ever touching the car's phone.

The 1993 models added a passenger-side airbag and automatic locking restrainer belts for front and rear seats. The system for the rear makes it easier to install child seats.

Lexus coupes are designed for people who want some of the feel of a sports car, along with the luxuries normally found only in large family sedans.

	Lexus SC 400	Lexus SC 300
Engine type	90 degree V-8	in-line 6
Displacement	4.0 liters	3.0 liters
Horsepower	250 at 5000 rpm	225 at 6000 rpm
Torque	260 lb-ft at 4400 rpm	210 lb-ft at 4800 rpm
Acceleration 0-60	6.9 seconds	7.4 seconds
Top track speed	150 mph	146 mph

CHAPTER 9

MAZDA: RX-7, BUILT FOR SPEED

Perhaps the Mazda RX-7, along with the classic Jaguar E-Type, is one of the few automobiles that qualify as a race car and street car at the same time.

In its racing-modified form, the RX-7 became, in 1991, the first Japanese-made car to win the Le Mans. The RX-7 had raced to other honors. In 1979, it won first and second places in its class in the Daytona endurance. The 1991 victory at Le Mans was its first full championship in a world-renowned race.

Mazda builds the RX-7 body around an engine that has no pistons, valves or lifters. RX-7 engineers were convinced that conventional engines waste power in converting the up-and-down motion of pistons into circular power necessary to turn wheels. So they powered the RX-7 with a rotary engine. The Mazda engine generates rotation without the need for a crankshaft.

This modified Mazda RX-7 racer won the 1991 Le Mans, coming in ahead of second and third placed Mercedes-Benz and Jaguar.

Rod Millen's RX-7 came in first in the Open Class at the 1991 Pikes Peak Hill Climb.

The results are impressive. The engine produces 255 horsepower at 6500 rpm, and 217 pound feet of torque at 5000 rpm. The RX-7 will go from zero to 60 mph in 4.9 seconds, making it one of the fastest sports cars on the road. Its top speed is 156 mph.

Compared to piston engines, the rotary design is recent, but it isn't new. The engine in the latest RX-7 has over 30 years of research and development behind it.

CHAPTER 10

MAZDA: RX-7, BUILT WITH PRECISION

Members of the RX-7 development team at Mazda all learned high-performance driving by getting behind the wheel and learning from professional drivers. That way, they had a better appreciation for the problems they were to solve in building a fast sports car.

The design team also used a supercomputer. One important way they used the computer was in reducing weight of the car so it could go faster.

A heavy car needs more power, so an important goal of the designers was to make the car as light as possible. The supercomputer showed designers where they could trim weight without loss of necessary strength.

The Mazda RX-7 rotary engine generates 255 horsepower at 6500 rpm.

At every point possible, Mazda engineers reduced the weight of the RX-7 by taking out unnecessary metal. They even took plugs of metal out of the brake and clutch pedals.

In pushing for the lightest car possible, engineers would eliminate a single gram of metal if they could. They bored out bits of metal even in small, unexpected places, such as on the brake and clutch pedals. They also took out metal from the support structure of the frame. They were careful to leave the supports strong enough to do their job.

The stick shift on the RX-7 is set so the driver's hand need move only inches from the steering wheel.

Engineers also considered safety in assembling the body. They built in special crumple places – areas that would crumple up in a severe wreck. By choosing where the car would cave in upon itself, they were able to build a safer area for driver and passengers.

CHAPTER 11

MAZDA: RX-7 R-1, STREET CAR AND RACER

Mazda makes a special version of the RX-7 for the purists who want a highway car that will handle almost exactly like a race car. It is called the RX-7 R-1.

It looks different from the RX-7, but not very different. The RX-7 R-1 has a wing across its back, just above the taillights. It also has a device called an "air dam" across the lower front. The air dam and the rear wing (often called a "spoiler") take advantage of air flow to keep the car stable when going high speeds.

Some unseen changes for the RX-7 R-1 include stiffer shock absorbers and an extra brace on the engine bay. These allow the car to handle S-curves and to corner like a race car.

This is the dash of a 1993 RX-7. Its designers preferred gauges to indicator lights.

Also, the engine of the RX-7 R-1 has an extra oil cooler, as well as air ducts to help cool the front brakes. The seats are covered with a special sport cloth that clings to clothing. The cloth holds the driver in place better during fast turns.

A race buff who wants the racer version of the RX-7 must give up some luxuries. The car does not come with a cruise control or with automatic transmission. The RX-7 R-1 comes only in yellow, red or black. The RX-7 R-1 is a stiffer, less luxurious car than the regular RX-7, but it runs like a real racer.

The 1993 RX-7 will go from zero to 60 mph in 4.9 seconds.

The RX-7 rotary engine in this 1993 model has a humming, winding sound that is different from sports cars with piston-driven engines.

CHAPTER 12

MAZDA: THE MX-3 AND MX-6

Mazda has a philosophy the company calls "Kansei Engineering." Kansei calls for meeting drivers' emotional needs while providing for their driving needs. Thus Mazda offers a large range of sports cars, and it works to make each as pleasing as possible.

It is the Kansei philosophy that caused Mazda engineers to spend hours "tuning" the sound of the MX-3 engine so it has a satisfying sports car sound.

The MX-3 comes in two models, both with rear seats, and both designed to be low-cost sports cars. The MX-3 GS has a 1.8 liter V-6 engine that delivers 130 horsepower at 6500 rpm. The MX-3 has a 1.6 liter 4-cylinder engine with fuel injection. It generates only 88 horsepower, but the engine is more fuel-efficient.

Driven by an 88 horsepower engine, the MX-3 is small, sporty and economical to drive.

This MX-6 can go from zero to 60 mph in 7.5 seconds.

Like the MX-3, the Mazda MX-6 comes in two models: one with a 4-cylinder engine and one with a V-6. The V-6 model, called the MX-6 LS, can accelerate from zero to 60 in 7.5 seconds.

Mazda had its studios in California and Japan jointly design the MX-6. The car has a rear seat, making it more practical as a passenger car than the smaller Mazda Miata.

In trying to protect the environment from pollution by dangerous agents, MX-6 engineers eliminated asbestos from the brakes, clutch and head gasket. They also devised an air conditioner that uses less freon gas.

The MX-3 and MX-6 models are Mazda's contribution to lower-cost sports coupes.

CHAPTER 13

MAZDA: MX-5, THE MIATA

Sports car enthusiasts around the world have loved the Miata. It was introduced in the middle of 1989 as a 1990 model. Since then, the Miata has won over 50 automotive awards.

At 2,222 pounds, it is a small car, designed to be light and easy to maneuver. To make it feel and sound like a sports car, the engineers at Mazda designed a racer's transmission. The stick shift has short linkage. You have to move the stick only 1.8 inches in shifting gears.

Engineers also gave much attention to the sound of the car. They wanted the muffler to sound like an exotic sports car. They tried over 100 different exhaust sounds before choosing one that had the right pitch. Drivers like to use the exhaust sound as a clue for when to shift gears.

This 1993 Mazda Miata comes in only four colors: red, white, black and blue.

Mazda MX-5: the Miata	
Engine type	In-line 4-cylinder
Displacement	1597cc (97 cubic inches)
Horsepower	116 at 6000 rpm
Torque	100 lb-ft at 5500 rpm

The car is a convertible, but it has an optional hardtop similar to the one used by the original classic Thunderbird. The hardtop snaps in place with little effort, making the Miata a fun car for all kinds of weather.

Mazda engineers kept the Miata light by using the same technology developed in trimming weight from the RX-7. They also made the Miata lighter by designing an aluminum hood and putting a lightweight battery in the trunk.

The interior of this 1993 Miata is made even more attractive by a sound system with five amplifiers and eight speakers.

CHAPTER 14

JAPANESE SPORTS CARS: IMPORTANT DATES

1969 Datsun 240 Z introduced in the United States.

1974 Datsun 260 Z comes out with rear seats and a longer wheelbase.

1975 Datsun introduces the 280 Z.

1979 Modified Mazda RX-7 racers win first and second in their class at Daytona.

1983 Nissan redesigns the Z body in the 300 ZX model.

1986 The Nissan 300 ZX is built smaller, ending the trend to make the Z series larger luxury cars.

1989 Mazda introduces the MX-5, called the Miata, as a 1990 model.

1991 A modified Mazda RX-7 wins at Le Mans; a Mazda RX-7 wins the Pikes Peak Hill Climb; Mitsubishi introduces the 3000 GT.

1992 *Motor Trend* magazine selects the Lexus 400 SC as Import Car of the Year.

1993 Most Japanese sports cars offer numerous safety features, including anti-lock brakes, air bags, and computer-controlled suspension systems for stability.

Moving into the next century: Japanese car makers will continue to pride themselves in being leaders in developing ways to build computer technology into their cars. So long as the American drivers are willing to buy fast, fun cars filled with high-tech equipment, the Japanese will continue to design, build and export them to America.

The Mitsubishi 3000 GT SL has front wheel drive.

The 1993 Nissan 300 ZX is designed for driver and passenger comfort.

GLOSSARY

air dam – A device on the front of a car that catches air and directs it in a way to give the car more stability; the Mazda RX-7 R-1 uses an air dam.

Datsun – The name Nissan used to market its cars in the United States in the 1970s and early 1980s.

exotic – A word often applied to a hand-assembled, low-production sports car.

fastback – A car design that slants the top of the roof directly to the rear bumper.

grand touring car – A large car as opposed to a sports car.

Kansei Engineering – The term Mazda uses to name their car-designing philosophy of paying attention to motorists' emotional needs as well as their driving needs.

Kelly Bluebook – A directory of used car prices for car dealers.

low-production car – A limited-production car, as opposed to one that is mass-produced.

mph – Miles per hour.

purists – People who want sports cars built only for speed and performance, not for luxury or comfort.

rpm – Revolutions per minute.

spoiler – A wing across the back of a car that makes use of air flow to help give the car stability.

straight six – An engine with six cylinders in a straight line.

turbocharged engine – An engine that has increased power because of a device that forces more air into the combustion chamber, allowing more fuel to burn, which drives the pistons with greater force.

INDEX